DATE DUE

DATE DUE	BORROWER'S NAME	ROOM NO.
	Melchur, Katherine	
	~~DEC 1 8 1997~~	
	~~MAY 2 7 1999~~	

591
KER
    Kerrod, Robin
     Animal life

LET'S INVESTIGATE SCIENCE
SCIENCE
Animal Life

LET'S INVESTIGATE SCIENCE
Animal Life

Robin Kerrod

Illustrated by Ted Evans

MARSHALL CAVENDISH
NEW YORK · LONDON · TORONTO · SYDNEY

Library Edition Published 1994

© Marshall Cavendish Corporation 1994

Published by Marshall Cavendish Corporation
2415 Jerusalem Avenue
PO Box 587
North Bellmore
New York 11710

Series created by Graham Beehag Book Design

Library of Congress Cataloging-in-Publication Data

Kerrod, Robin.
    Let's investigate animal life / Robin Kerrod; illustrated by
Ted Evans. -- Library ed.
    p. cm. -- (Let's investigate science)
Includes bibliographical references and index.
Summary: Investigates animal biology, examining the main animal groups
and how they fit into different environments.
ISBN 1-85435-623-2   ISBN 1-85435-620-8 (set)
1. Animals -- Juvenile literature. 2. Habitat (Ecology) -- Juvenile literature
[1. Animals. 2. Animals -- Habitat.]
I. Evans, Ted ill. II. Title. III. Title: Animal life.
IV. Series: Kerrod, Robin. Let's investigate science.
QL49.K43 1994   93-4483
591--dc20   CIP
                                                        AC

MCC Editorial Consultant: Marvin Tolman, Ed.D.
                           Brigham Young University

Printed and bound in Hong Kong

Contents

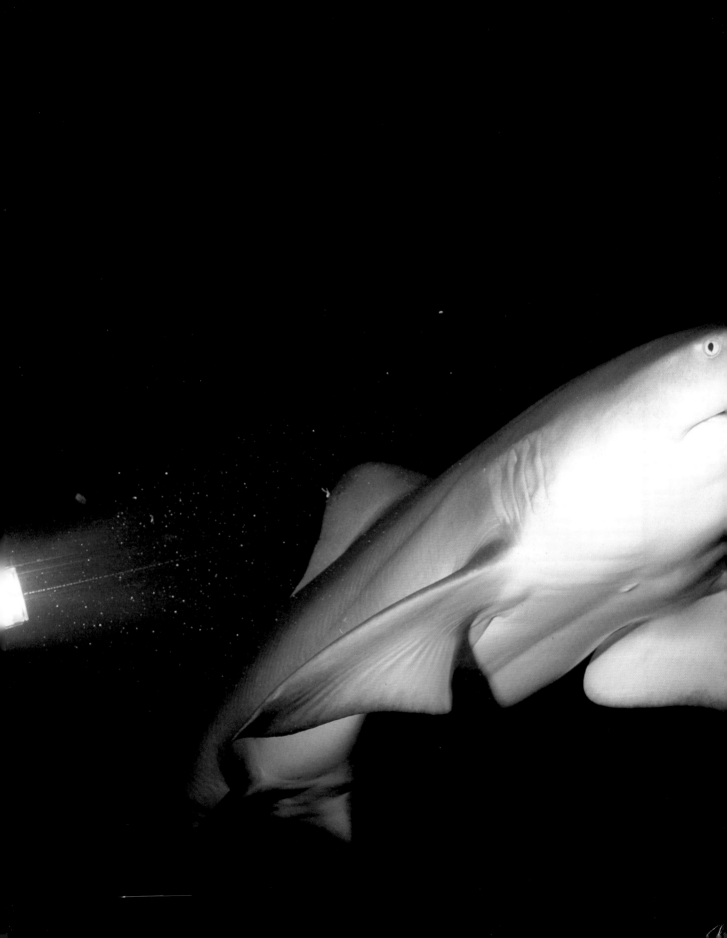

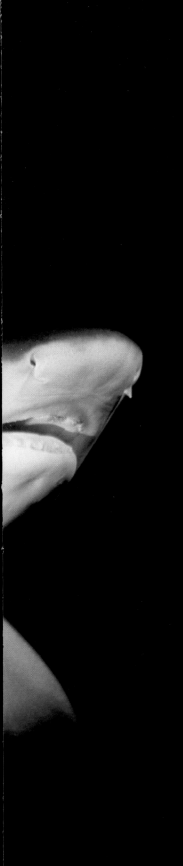

Introduction

The world around us is made up of millions of different kinds of things – rocks, trees, birds, and so on. But there is a world of difference between rocks, trees, and birds. Rocks are not alive. Trees and birds are.

We can divide everything on Earth into two basic groups, living things and non-living things. Living things differ from non-living things in a number of ways. But the key difference is that they can reproduce, or produce more of their own kind. Non-living things can't.

Just as the natural world can be divided into two parts – the living and non-living – so can the living world be split into two parts – plants and animals. Usually it is quite easy to tell plants from animals. Plants usually stay where they are, while animals move around. Plants have no organs, such as eyes and ears, to sense their surroundings in the same way that animals do. But a key difference between plants and animals is that plants can make their own food, while animals can't.

In all there are millions of different kinds of animals, from tiny creatures you can see only under a microscope to gigantic creatures like the Blue whale, which can tip the scales at up to 200 tons (190 tonnes). In this book we investigate animal biology, looking at the main animal groups to see how they fit into different environments.

You can check your answers to the questions featured throughout this book on pages 60-61.

Note: *Unless stated, the animals depicted in the illustrations are not drawn to scale.*

◀ **This Lemon shark is native of the west Atlantic Ocean. It can grow up to about 11 feet (3.5 meters) long.**

1 Animal Biology

◀ A Great blue heron in its watery habitat. When hunting, it stands quite still. Only its eyes move as it seeks its prey, such as a frog or a fish. When it spies one, its sharp bill shoots out with lightning speed and is almost always on target.

In this chapter we look at the basic processes behind animal life, the way animals sense their environment, and the way they reproduce their own kind.

To stay alive, all animals must eat. The food they eat provides them with the energy they need to grow and move around. It also provides them with body-building materials.

All animals must breathe. They need to take in oxygen from their surroundings to "burn" their food and so produce energy.

To search for food or to escape from enemies, animals must make the best of their senses, using their eyes, ears, nose, and so on, to keep them aware of what is happening around them.

Animals also need their senses to find a mate so that they will be able to reproduce. The process of finding a mate, reproducing, and raising offspring occupies a large part of an animal's life.

▼ The cheetah is the fastest animal on land, able to reach a speed of 60 mph (96 km/h) or more in short bursts. To achieve such speeds, it "burns up" energy at a fast rate. It lives on a high-energy diet of meat from the prey it kills.

Q What is an animal that eats meat called?

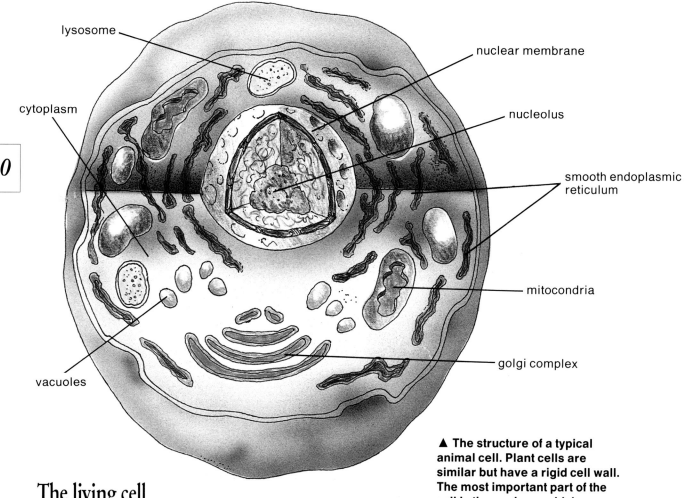

lysosome

nuclear membrane

cytoplasm

nucleolus

10

smooth endoplasmic reticulum

mitocondria

golgi complex

vacuoles

▲ **The structure of a typical animal cell. Plant cells are similar but have a rigid cell wall. The most important part of the cell is the nucleus, which controls the other parts of the cell.**

The living cell

The bodies of all living things – plants as well as animals – are made up of basic units called cells. Mostly, cells are very small and can be seen only under a microscope. Typically, it would take 4,000 side by side to measure an inch (about 1,600 to measure a centimeter).

The simplest animals, like the amoeba, are made up of just a single cell. But most animals are made up of literally millions of cells. In an animal's body there are many different types of cells that have a specialist role to play in the way the body works. Groups of similar types of cells make up the different body tissues and organs.

How the cell works

Although there are many types of cells, they all have a similar basic structure. The picture above shows roughly

Prison walls

The first person to see a cell was an English scientist named Robert Hooke in the 1600s. He was one of the pioneers of the microscope. Hook gave the name "cell" to the basic units of living things because he compared them to prison cells.

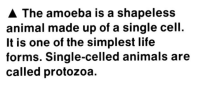

what a typical cell would look like if you saw it close-up. It is enclosed in a protective skin, the cell membrane. This nevertheless lets materials move into and out of the cell.

The bulk of the cell is made up of a jellylike material called cytoplasm. Within this are various structures, each of which has a role to play in the working of the cell. The most important structure is the nucleus. This is the "brains" of the cell that controls its other parts. Some parts called the endoplasmic reticulum make complex substances, such as body-building proteins. Other parts called the mitochondria produce the cell's energy.

11

▲ The amoeba is a shapeless animal made up of a single cell. It is one of the simplest life forms. Single-celled animals are called protozoa.

The "plans"

The nucleus contains thread-like bodies called chromosomes. They carry units called genes, which we can think of as "plans" for the various parts of the body. In each cell of the body, the nucleus tells the cell to work according to these plans.

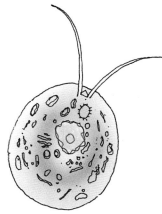

▲ This is another protozoan. It has a definite shape, and it moves itself around by means of the two whiplike flagella.

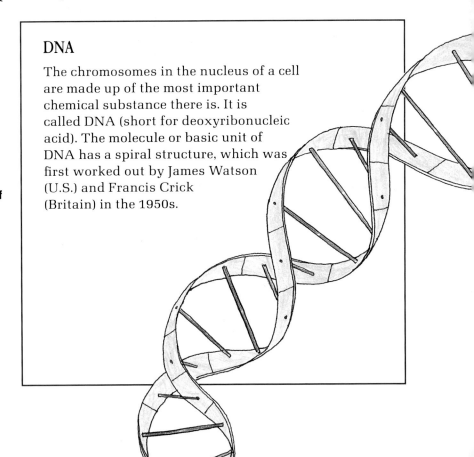

DNA

The chromosomes in the nucleus of a cell are made up of the most important chemical substance there is. It is called DNA (short for deoxyribonucleic acid). The molecule or basic unit of DNA has a spiral structure, which was first worked out by James Watson (U.S.) and Francis Crick (Britain) in the 1950s.

► The horse is a typical herbivore, or plant-eater. It spends most of its time eating, grazing on grass.

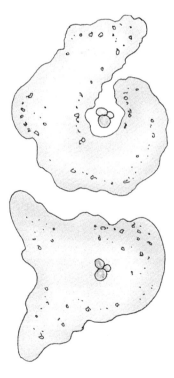

▲ The amoeba has no special organs for feeding. When it comes across a food particle, it flows around it and absorbs any nutrients. Any waste is left behind as the amoeba flows away.

Feeding

Animals must eat regularly if they are to survive. The food provides them with energy and the essential materials their bodies need. Animals can't make their own food like plants can, however. Therefore they have to eat plants or other animals.

The main substances in food are carbohydrates such as sugar, fats, and proteins. Carbohydrates are the main energy-providers. Fats are an efficient way of storing energy. And proteins are needed to build up body tissues. In addition, small amounts of minerals and vitamins are needed to keep a body healthy.

The plant eaters

Many animal species including rabbits, deer, cattle, sheep, and horses eat mainly plant materials and are called herbivores. The majority of herbivores are grazers, which feed on grass. But other herbivores such as goats are browsers, feeding on shrubs, shoots, and branches as well.

Plant materials are made up mainly of cellulose, which is hard to digest. Many herbivores have a special digestive system which can handle these materials. Grazing animals such as deer and cattle have a stomach with many chambers. One is called the rumen, and the animals are known as ruminants.

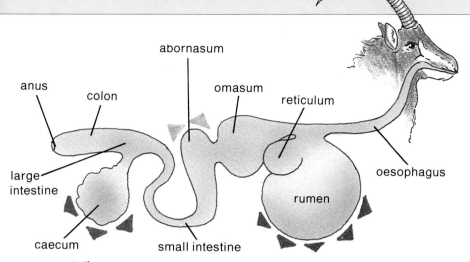

anus
colon
abornasum
omasum
reticulum
large intestine
oesophagus
rumen
caecum
small intestine

◄ When a ruminant feeds, the food passes first into a chamber called the rumen, where it is partly digested. Then it is returned to the mouth as a "cud," which is chewed for some time. The chewing and attack by digestive juices break the food down further and it is then reswallowed. It passes in turn through the other stomach chambers and into the gut, where the food substances are absorbed.

The meat-eaters

Animals that eat meat are called carnivores. They include lions, cats, dogs, snakes, and sharks. Meat-eaters have a great advantage over plant-eaters because meat is a concentrated food compared with plant material. Carnivores therefore do not need to eat as often. Whereas an antelope must spend most of its waking hours feeding, a lion need only feed well about once a week!

Most meat-eaters prey on live animals, but some live on dead ones, or carrion. Vultures and hyenas are among the animals that feed on carrion.

Some animals feed on a variety of both plant and animal materials. They are classed as omnivores. They are among the most successful animals because they can exploit whatever food source they find. Cockroaches and rats are omnivorous. So are we humans.

▲ The sloth is renowned as one of the slowest of animals. This is because it eats only woody materials that provide it with little energy. Its average speed on the ground is only one-tenth of a mile per hour (0.16 km/h)!

◄ A lion feeds on a fresh "kill." Lions are the top carnivores of the African savanna, feeding on Gazelle, Wildebeest, and other antelopes.

Breathing

Like feeding, breathing is something all animals must do, whether they live in the air, on land, underground, or underwater. Breathing is the means by which animals take in oxygen. They must take in oxygen to "burn" their food and produce energy. The burning, or oxidation process, produces carbon dioxide as a waste product. This whole process of taking in oxygen and giving out carbon dioxide is called respiration.

Simple animals such as the amoeba and jellyfish have no special breathing apparatus. They absorb the little oxygen they need from the water they live in.

The more advanced animals require special breathing organs and a means of getting oxygen to all the body cells.

Lungs

In mammals, birds, and reptiles, the breathing organs are the lungs. They are balloon-like bags, lined with little pockets, or sacs, of spongy tissue with thin walls.

The oxygen in the air breathed into the lungs passes through the sac walls into fine blood vessels, and the blood carries it to all the body cells. The blood also carries back to the lungs dissolved carbon dioxide gas. This passes out into the air and is breathed out.

▶ **The lungs are made up of little "bags," or sacs, like this. Through its thin walls, oxygen passes into the fine blood vessels (red) and carbon dioxide passes out from others (blue).**

14

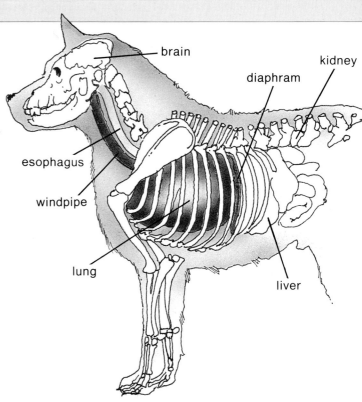

brain
kidney
diaphram
esophagus
windpipe
lung
liver

▲ **Like all mammals, a dog breathes through lungs. It breathes in and out by contracting and relaxing a large sheet of muscle called the diaphragm. All mammals breathe in and out in this way.**

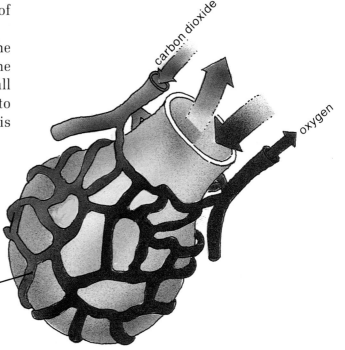

carbon dioxide

oxygen

capillaries

► This is the inside of the body of a grasshopper, a typical insect. The body is riddled by a network of tiny tubes, which connect with holes at the sides of the body. Air passes through these holes, called spiracles, into the tubes. Oxygen then passes directly from the air into the surrounding tissues.

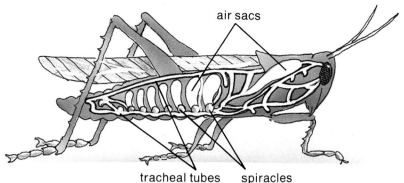

air sacs

tracheal tubes   spiracles

15

The birds and the bees

Birds need a great deal of energy to fly and have a particularly efficient lung system. Their lungs are connected to a set of chambers called air sacs. When a bird breathes in, all the air in the lung is changed, giving the bird the maximum amount of oxygen. Because the lungs of other animals are enclosed, not all of the air in them is exchanged each time they breathe.

Bees and all the other insects have quite a different method of breathing. They have no lungs, but breath through holes in the sides of their bodies.

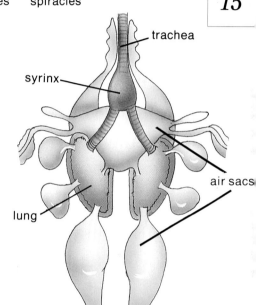

trachea

syrinx

air sacs

lung

Breathing in water

Many animals live in water, such as whales, dolphins, and seals, are mammals. They have lungs and have to come to the surface regularly to breathe in air. But fish and shellfish breathe in the water through organs called gills.

Breathing through gills

Fish breathe underwater through gills. The gills are feathery organs rich in blood vessels. They are located in the head and are connected to the mouth. To breathe, the fish opens its mouth and takes in water. It then closes its mouth and expels the water past the gills and out through the gill slits. Oxygen passes from the water into the blood passing through the gills, while the carbon dioxide passes in the opposite direction.

Senses

Like us, animals gain information about their surroundings by means of their senses. Simple animals have very primitive senses. For example, they may just respond to light or to touch. The higher animals rely on the same senses as we do – sight, hearing, smell, touch, and taste. Some animals have other senses as well.

The main senses animals use are their sight, hearing, and smell but they do not always use them equally. A bird like a hawk, for example, relies mostly on sight. Its eyes act rather like a telescope to spot tiny prey on the ground while the bird is still high in the air.

Smell and hearing

Dogs rely more on their sense of smell than their eyesight. This is why they are always sniffing things. Dogs also have an acute sense of hearing. They can hear sounds that we can't because their ears are sensitive to very high pitched sounds.

Bats cannot only hear such "ultrasonic" sounds, they can also make them. They do this to help them navigate in the air. They send out ultrasonic signals and listen for an echo. If there is one, there is an obstacle – or a meal! – in their path.

16

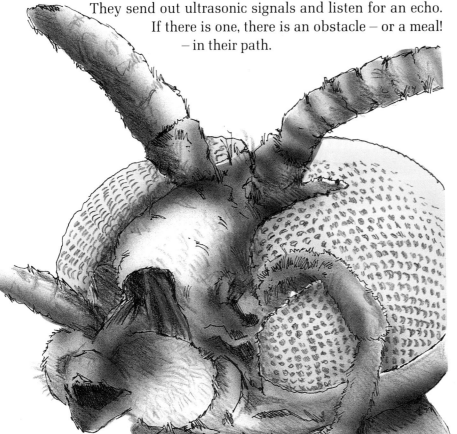

▼ This animal is a mammal called a tarsier, which lives in the rain forests of Southeast Asia. It has huge owl-like eyes.

Q 1. What does this tell us about its way of life?

◄ This "thing from outer space" is actually the head of a small fly, highly magnified. The colored "domes" are its compound eyes, made up of tens of thousands of separate lenses.

▼ This is a cat's eye. All members of the cat family – lions, tigers, and so on, have eyes like this.

Q 2. In what ways do cats' eyes differ from our own?

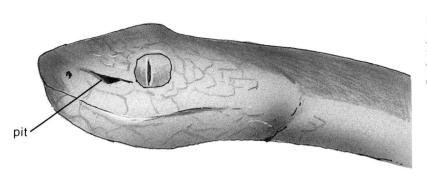

pit

◄ Rattlesnakes and other pit vipers have an opening, or pit, just in front of each eye. It is sensitive to heat, which enables them to hunt live prey in the dark.

Special senses

The heat-sensitive "pit" of the rattlesnake and other pit vipers (above) is an example of special senses certain animals have developed.

One of the great wonders of nature is bird migration. They often fly thousands of miles between their summer and winter homes. They use the Sun and the stars to navigate, but also appear to have some kind of body "compass." Experiments have indeed shown that birds have certain cells that are sensitive to the Earth's magnetism.

In Australia, some species of termite also seem to sense the Earth's magnetism because they usually build their nests in a north-south direction. They are known as compass termites.

▲ Mice usually search for food at night. Their whiskers help them sense their surroundings.

Q 1. What sense are they using?

▼ Moths have feathery feelers, or antennae, to sense their surroundings.

Q 2. What sense are they using?

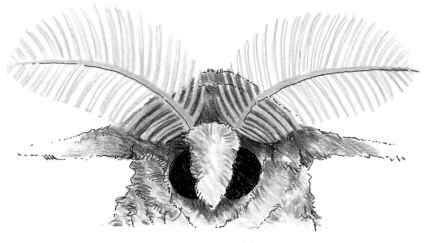

Reproduction

The ability to reproduce, or produce more of their own kind, is one of the basic characteristics of all living things.

Most animals reproduce sexually. A male and a female animal get together, or mate, so that their sex cells can join and create new life. The male sex cells are called sperm, the female sex cells eggs. The coming together of the sex cells is called fertilization.

In fish and amphibians, fertilization takes place outside the animals' bodies. The females lay their eggs in the water, and then the male releases its sperm to fertilize them. The young of amphibians such as frogs change their body form as they grow; this is an example of metamorphosis. Insects undergo metamorphosis, too, changing their body form a number of times as they develop from egg to adult.

In reptiles and birds, fertilization takes place inside the female's body. The female then lays fertilized eggs, from which the young eventually hatch. Fertilization is internal in mammals, too. But the eggs stay inside the females and grow into young there. After the young are born, the mother feeds them on milk she produces.

18

Changing form

In higher animals, the young hatch from eggs or are born as tiny versions of adult animals. But in amphibians and insects, the creature that hatches from the egg is quite different in form from the adult. It changes from one form to the other in a number of stages. This process is called metamorphosis.

A frog egg hatches into a wriggling tadpole, which breathes with gills. Gradually it develops legs and changes into a frog.

An insect egg hatches into a larva, or caterpillar, which then changes into a pupa, from which the adult emerges.

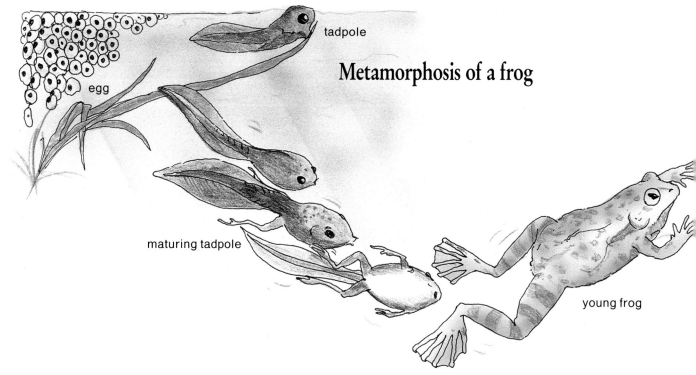

tadpole

Metamorphosis of a frog

egg

maturing tadpole

young frog

Metamorphosis of a butterfly

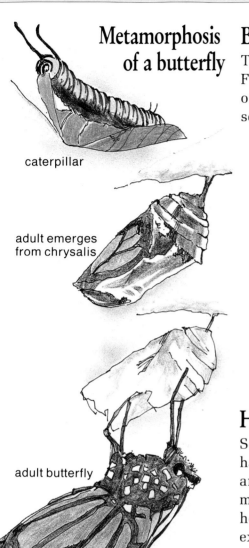

caterpillar

adult emerges from chrysalis

adult butterfly

Budding

Tiny water creatures called hydra reproduce by budding. From time to time a swelling, or bud, develops somewhere on the body and grows into a replica of the parent. Then it separates to pursue an independent life.

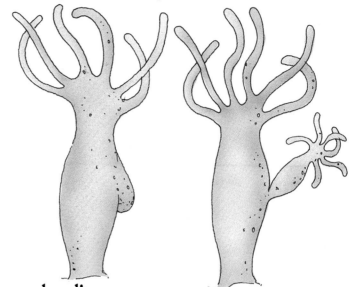

Hermaphrodites

Some simple animals, including worms and snails, do not have separate sexes. Each individual has both male and female sex organs. Such animals are called hermaphrodites. These animals can't mate with themselves, however! They must pair with another individual, and exchange sperm with it. They then both go away and produce eggs.

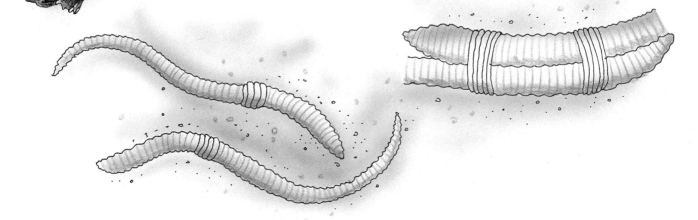

2
Animal Groups

◄ **These delightful creatures are Ring-tailed lemurs, which live in the forests of Madagascar, an island off eastern Africa. Lemurs are found nowhere else in the world. They belong to the same animal group as humans – they are primates.**

One of the main tasks of the scientist is to bring some kind of order into the apparent chaos of the world around us. For example, the chemist classifies the chemical elements into groups with similar properties. But there are only about 90 different elements.

Pity the poor zoologist, then, who has to try to bring order into the animal kingdom, in which there are more than a million different kinds of animals!

Biologists have been working on the problem of classifying living things – plants as well as animals – for over 300 years. The modern system of classification was pioneered by the Swedish biologist Carolus Linnaeus in the mid-1700s. It divides animals into a series of groups, broadly speaking, according to their anatomy or structure.

If you turn the page you will see a kind of "family tree" of animals, based on this system of grouping. In the rest of the chapter we look at the essential features of the main animal groups.

▼ **This is a whale shark, which can reach a length of over 40 feet (12 meters). It feeds on plankton, like a whale, but it is a fish – the worlds biggest, in fact. The diver illustrated with the shark is drawn to scale.**

Q **Whales belong to an animal group that is quite different from fish. What is it?**

The family tree

Here is one way we can look at the animal kingdom as a whole, as a kind of tree with branches. The main part of the tree is occupied by creatures that have soft bodies and no backbones. We call them invertebrates. They make up most of the animal kingdom. The most advanced invertebrates are animals with jointed bodies, such as insects and spiders.

The more advanced animals have a bony skeleton and a backbone. We call them vertebrates. They include fish, amphibians, reptiles, birds, and mammals. We human beings are mammals. So are bats and bears, horses and groundhogs, whales and walruses.

22

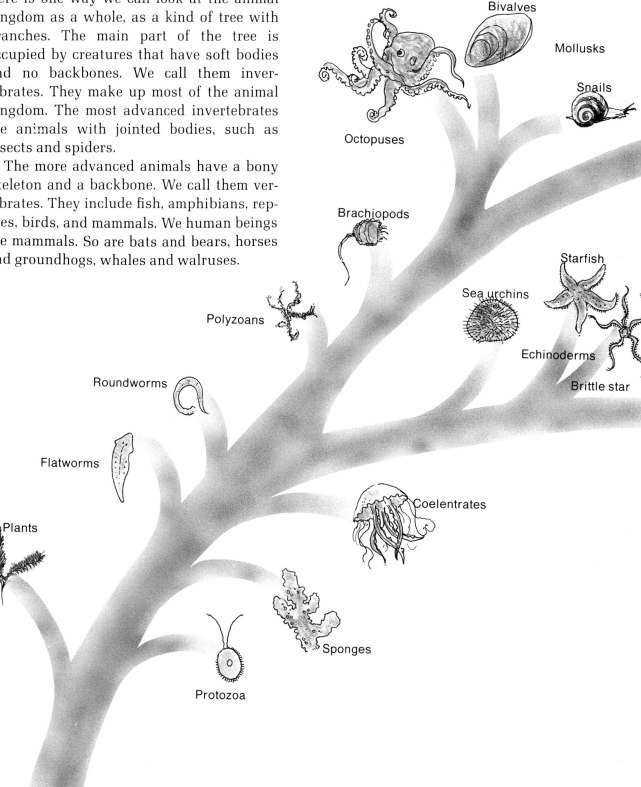

Bivalves

Mollusks

Snails

Octopuses

Brachiopods

Starfish

Sea urchins

Echinoderms

Brittle star

Polyzoans

Roundworms

Coelentrates

Flatworms

Plants

Sponges

Protozoa

Animal species

Broadly speaking, we talk about species of animal, meaning kinds of animals. But "species" has a specialized meaning. It is the narrowest grouping in animal classification.

Several species of similar animals form a larger group called a "genus." Several genera form a still larger group called a "family;" several families form an "order;" several orders form a "class;" several classes form a "phylum;" and several phyla make up the animal kingdom.

Centipedes

Insects

Spiders

Arthropods

Crustaceans

Trilobites

Leeches

Bristleworms

Earthworms

Annelids

Protochordates

Amphibians

Reptiles

Lungfish

Fish

Cod

Sharks

Birds

Vertebrates

Mammals

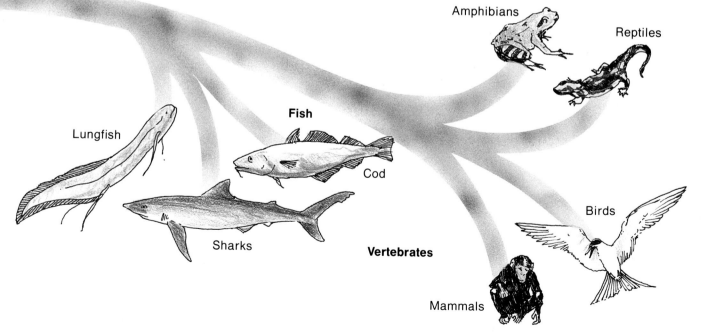

24

Simple life

Under this title we include a very broad range of creatures. Some, like the sponges, for example, don't seem like animals at all. Sponges live, fixed to the seabed, in warm climates. They draw in water through holes in their simple, spongy bodies. Any food particles are removed and digested in a central body cavity.

We call sponges sessile animals – ones that cannot move. Sea anemones are another group of sessile animals. They have tiny waving tentacles, which trap swimming animals, even small fish, for food. Corals are similar, but they build a skeleton of limestone around them. The skeletons of billions of corals in time can build up to form coral reefs and islands.

Worms and leeches

Worms of many kinds are found all over. Most familiar is the earthworm, which is found in most soils. In the sea are colorful flatworms and fanworms. Fanworms filter out food from the water with tentacles, much like corals.

Some flatworms are parasites – they live inside other animals. They include tapeworms, which are sometimes found in humans. They can grow up to 30 feet (9 meters) long! Leeches are another kind of wormlike creature that live on the blood they suck from other animals.

Some of the simple life found in the oceans. The jellyfish has a nearly transparent body that looks rather like an umbrella. Its long, trailing tentacles are covered with stinging cells to paralyze the tiny creatures it feeds on.

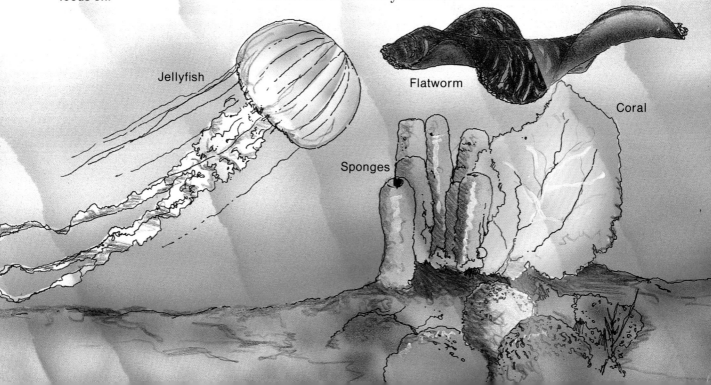

Jellyfish

Flatworm

Coral

Sponges

Shelled mollusks

Other invertebrates have their soft bodies enclosed in shells. The most familiar example is the garden snail. It is noted for its muscular foot, on which it slides around, lubricating its path with slime. Many snails live in water. Other water mollusks include scallops and oysters. They are called bivalves because they have two parts to their shells.

25

INVESTIGATE

You can study the habits of earthworms by building a worm farm. You can make one using a clear plastic open-topped jar or large bottle. To see what worms do in soil, fill the jar with layers of different material, such as soil, sand, and peat. Place dead leaves and grass on top. Find some ordinary earthworms and drop them into your wormery. Water it, then put it in the dark. Check your worm farm every day to see what, if anything, has happened.

▲ An ordinary garden snail is dwarfed by an African giant snail. This giant can measure up to 16 inches (40 cm) long.

▼ Octopus and cuttlefish are also mollusks, although they don't have an external shell. The cuttlefish has a chalky plate inside its body.

Q These two animals, and also squid, propel themselves in quite a different way from other sea creatures. What do they do?

Octopus

▼ The starfish is a rough-skinned predator that preys on mollusks.

Cuttlefish

Starfish

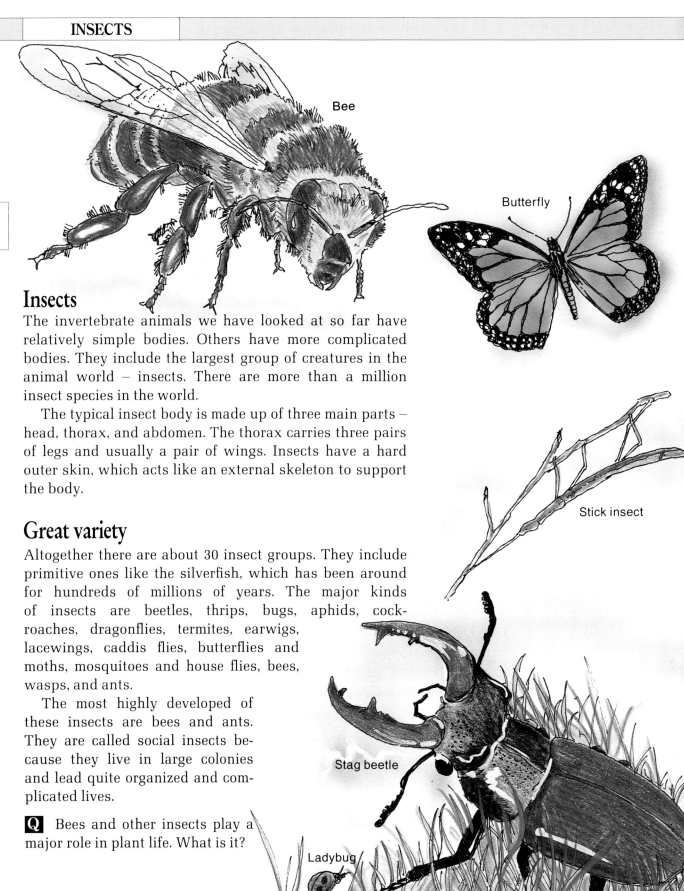

Bee

Butterfly

Stick insect

Stag beetle

Ladybug

26

Insects

The invertebrate animals we have looked at so far have relatively simple bodies. Others have more complicated bodies. They include the largest group of creatures in the animal world – insects. There are more than a million insect species in the world.

The typical insect body is made up of three main parts – head, thorax, and abdomen. The thorax carries three pairs of legs and usually a pair of wings. Insects have a hard outer skin, which acts like an external skeleton to support the body.

Great variety

Altogether there are about 30 insect groups. They include primitive ones like the silverfish, which has been around for hundreds of millions of years. The major kinds of insects are beetles, thrips, bugs, aphids, cockroaches, dragonflies, termites, earwigs, lacewings, caddis flies, butterflies and moths, mosquitoes and house flies, bees, wasps, and ants.

The most highly developed of these insects are bees and ants. They are called social insects because they live in large colonies and lead quite organized and complicated lives.

Q Bees and other insects play a major role in plant life. What is it?

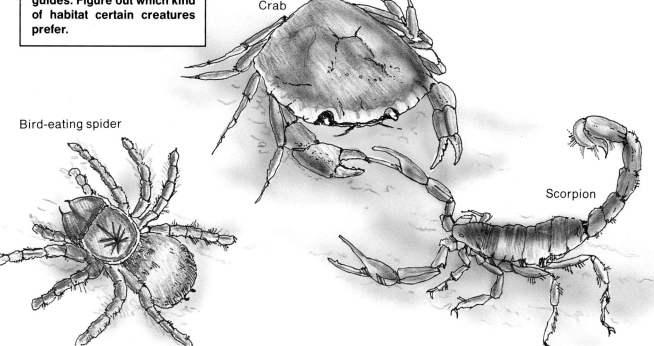

► These tiny creatures are dust mites, too small for the eye to see. They are found in the home, particularly in blankets, where they feed on the flakes of dead skin that we humans shed all the time. They are quite harmless, although they can cause allergies in some people.

Q 1. These mites are not insects. How can we tell?

INVESTIGATE

It is not difficult to find insects, spiders, and other arthropods. Look under a stone, in the leaves under trees, under rotting vegetation, and you are bound to see some – scurrying beetles, centipedes and millipedes, ground beetles, ants, and maybe their nest with hundreds of little white eggs.

Investigate different places and make a note of which little creatures you find. Try to identify them from field guides. Figure out which kind of habitat certain creatures prefer.

Other arthropods

Insects have jointed legs. They are part of a large group of animals with jointed legs called arthropods. The most familiar of the other arthropods are the spiders. Closely related to them are scorpions, noted for their curved stinging tail. Most scorpions are desert-dwellers, that sting their prey to death. Some are deadly enough to kill humans.

Another group of arthropods are the crustaceans, most of which live in water. Crabs and lobsters are typical crustaceans, with a hard outer covering to their body. The smaller crustaceans, such as shrimp and krill, are part of the diet of many other animals, from small fish to huge whales.

Q 2. There is a fundamental difference between insects and other arthropods. Look at the pictures on this page and see if you can spot what this difference is.

Crab

Bird-eating spider

Scorpion

Fish and amphibians

Fish were the first vertebrates to develop, some 500 million years ago. Today there are some 20,000 species. Fish are superbly adapted for their life in the water. They have a typical shape, that we call streamlined. This shape creates the least resistance when fish swim through the water.

28

An essential feature of a typical fish is the air or swim bladder. This is an air-filled sac that helps the fish maintain its buoyancy or position in the water.

Sharks, however, have no air bladder. They stay up in the water because their stiff fins act like wings to create "lift."

There is another major difference between ordinary fish and sharks. Ordinary fish have a bony skeleton. A shark's skeleton is made up of a gristly material called cartilage instead of bone.

Q Like all living things fish must breathe to stay alive. How do they breathe underwater?

▼ The angler fish lives in deep, dark waters. It is so called because it dangles from its head a luminous lure as bait to attract smaller fish to eat.

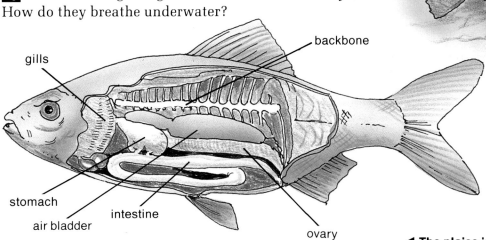

gills
backbone
stomach
air bladder
intestine
ovary

◄ The plaice is one kind of flatfish, that lives flat on the seabed. When it first hatches from the egg, the plaice has eyes on opposite sides of the head, like most other fish. But as the fish grows, one eye moves around until both are on the top as it lies flat on the ocean floor.

Amphibians

Amphibians were the first vertebrates to leave the water and live on land about 400 million years ago. But amphibians have not completely forsaken water. They spend much of their time around water and return to it to breed.

The most familiar kinds of amphibians are frogs and toads, which are found in damp habitats throughout the world. Other amphibians include salamanders and newts. One of the most interesting kinds of salamander is the mudpuppy, which is notable for its external gills.

Some amphibians are highly poisonous, including the fire salamander and the poison arrow frogs of South America. Most of them are brightly colored to warn other animals that they are dangerous to eat.

INVESTIGATE

If you live near a pond where there are frogs (or toads), you can study firsthand the amazing way their eggs develop into tadpoles, which then transform into baby frogs. As soon as the frogs spawn in the spring, collect a little of the jellylike spawn and keep it in water in an aquarium or large bowl with some water weed. Change the water every few days, preferably replacing it with fresh pond water. Keep a daily record of the changes that take place in the spawn.

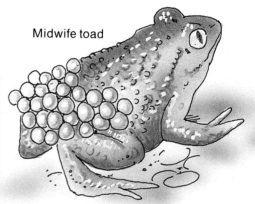

Midwife toad

Tailed frog

Red poison
arrow frog

Mudpuppy

Reptiles

Reptiles include three main groups of animals: snakes and lizards, tortoises and turtles, alligators and crocodiles. They have better lungs and stronger legs than amphibians and are therefore better adapted to life on land. Their bodies are covered with tough, waterproof scales. But like amphibians, reptiles are cold-blooded.

30

Q 1. Most reptiles are found in warm climates. Why?

▼ **The tree python is a type of snake called a constrictor. It winds itself around its prey and crushes it to death.**

▲ **The cobra is one of the so-called "hooded" snakes, which have the habit of flattening their neck when frightened or excited. They are among the most deadly of the poisonous snakes.**

Egg layers

Most reptiles reproduce by laying eggs from which their young hatch. But some species give birth to living young. The harmless garter snake, found throughout the U.S., is one of them.

Q 2. Reptiles can't incubate their eggs by sitting on them like birds do. Why can't they?

IT'S AMAZING!

Snakes can swallow prey wider than their own body. This is because they can unhinge their lower jaw and thus open their mouth very wide.

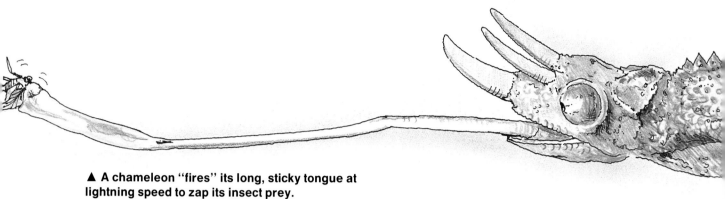

▲ A chameleon "fires" its long, sticky tongue at lightning speed to zap its insect prey.

Snakes and lizards

This is the largest reptile group. Snakes vary in size from a few inches to more than 30 feet (9 meters), the length of the Reticulated python of Asia.

Several snakes are poisonous, including the coral snake and the rattlesnake, which are found widely in the Western deserts of the U.S.

The largest of the world's lizards lives on the Indonesian island of Komodo, and is known as the Komodo Dragon. It measures about 12 feet (3.6 meters) long. But most lizards are only a few inches long.

Q Millions of years ago "terrible lizards" ruled the world. What do we usually call these animals?

▲ The American side-necked turtle, or Helmeted turtle, lives in rivers and streams in South America. Turtles are among the most ancient living species, having existed on Earth for 75 million years.

◄ Both alligators (left) and crocodiles (below) are found in the the Florida Everglades.

breastbone

Birds

Birds differ from all the animals we have looked at so far because they are warm-blooded. This enables them to be very active and to survive even in very cold climates. Birds fly by using their wings. These provide both the forward force, or thrust, to propel them through the air, and the upward force, or lift, to keep their heavy bodies up in the air. The wings are specially shaped to develop lift. The feathers fit together to form a smooth surface for the air to flow over. A bird's bones are different from those of most animals. They are hollow, and have a honeycomb structure, which makes them strong but light. The breastbone is broad to allow for the attachment of the well-developed breast muscles, which the bird uses to flap its wings.

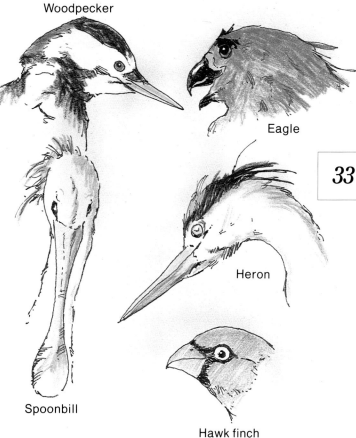

Woodpecker

Eagle

Heron

Spoonbill

Hawk finch

▲ **Brown pelicans abound in the Florida Keys. They fish by diving into the water from the air.**

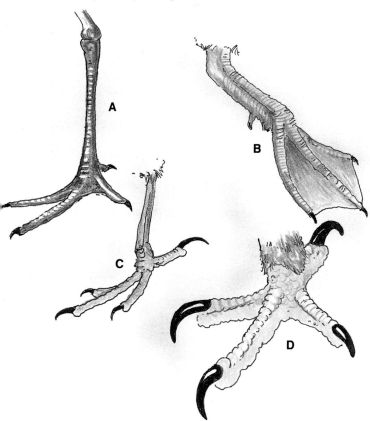

A

B

C

D

Bills and legs

We can tell a lot about a bird by looking at it bill (beak) and legs. The bill and legs give us an idea about how the bird feeds and where it lives.

The eagle has a strong, hooked bill for tearing the flesh of its prey. The heron stabs at fish and frogs with its long sharp bill. The woodpecker uses its chisel-like bill to bore holes. With its flat bill, the spoonbill sieves the mud for small creatures. The hawkfinch's bill is immensely strong and capable of cracking cherry pits.

Q In the pictures on the left these feet belong to birds that do different things. Identify which of the feet is suited to fishing, wading, swimming, and perching.

▲ The White-tailed possum is a native of Australia and New Zealand. It hangs from a branch with its prehensile, or grasping tail. It is a marsupial. A teaspoon could hold about 15 newborn possums!

▼ Piglets making a meal of it! Like all mammal mothers, the sow is feeding them with her milk.

Mammals

Mammals are the most advanced form of animal life. We human beings are mammals. So are dogs and cats, horses and rabbits, shrews and rhinoceroses, porcupines and elephants, and bats and whales.

Mammals have become successful for several reasons. They have relatively large brains, which enable them to learn quickly. They are warm-blooded and often covered with fur or hair. This enables them to live in all kinds of climates. Mammals give birth to live young and usually look after and protect the offspring until they are mature enough to look after themselves. The female feeds the young on milk from her mammary (breast) glands.

Types of mammals

Most mammals are placental mammals. The young grow inside the mother's womb, taking in nourishment through an organ called a placenta. They stay inside the mother for some time – 22 months in the case of an elephant!

In mammals called marsupials, however, the young are born in a very early stage of development. They then move to a kind of pouch on the mother's stomach, where they grow to maturity. The opossum, which is found widely in the southern United States, is a marsupial.

But the oddest mammals of all lay eggs! When they hatch, the mother feeds the young on her milk. An example of this type of mammal is the platypus (see page 49).

INVESTIGATE

Most wild mammals tend to be shy of humans and will run away or hide when they hear you coming. But they often leave footprints behind. Look for prints on muddy tracks and on the banks of ponds and streams. Sketch them, and then try to identify them from a field guide. You can make a plaster cast of the best ones using plaster of Paris. Most field guides will tell you how.

Feeding the animals

In all there are about 4,000 different kinds of mammals. About half of them are rodents, such as rats and squirrels, and about a quarter are bats. We sometimes group the mammals by what they eat. The carnivores, for example, eat mainly meat, the herbivores mainly vegetation, and the insectivores mainly insects.

Carnivores include dogs, cats, and bears; herbivores are grazing animals such as horses and antelope; and insectivores include bats and groundhogs.

Some animals will eat almost anything and are called omnivores. Human beings are omnivores.

▲ The tiger is a carnivore, which eats the meat of the prey it hunts.

▼ This spider monkey from South America is a primate, the same mammal group to which human beings belong. Note its prehensile tail.

▼ This disk-winged bat from Central America is a flying mammal.

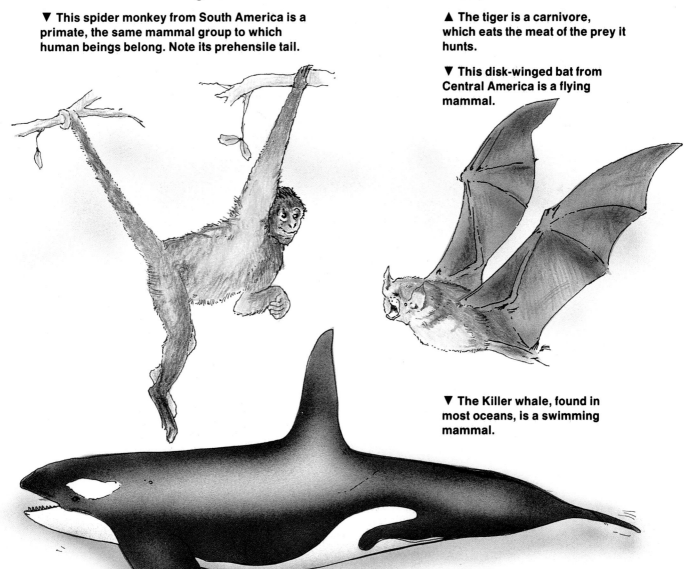

▼ The Killer whale, found in most oceans, is a swimming mammal.

Little and large

Over the past two to three million years the species Homo sapiens has become dominant in the mammal world. This species is the one to which you and all the rest of the human race belong. Translated, the species-name means "wise man." It reflects the fact that humans have larger brains than the other mammals and are much more intelligent.

Q One of the species illustrated in the picture is not a mammal. Which one is it, and to which other major group of animals does it belong?

36

Brachiosaurus –
the largest dinosaur.

The African elephant –
the largest land animal.

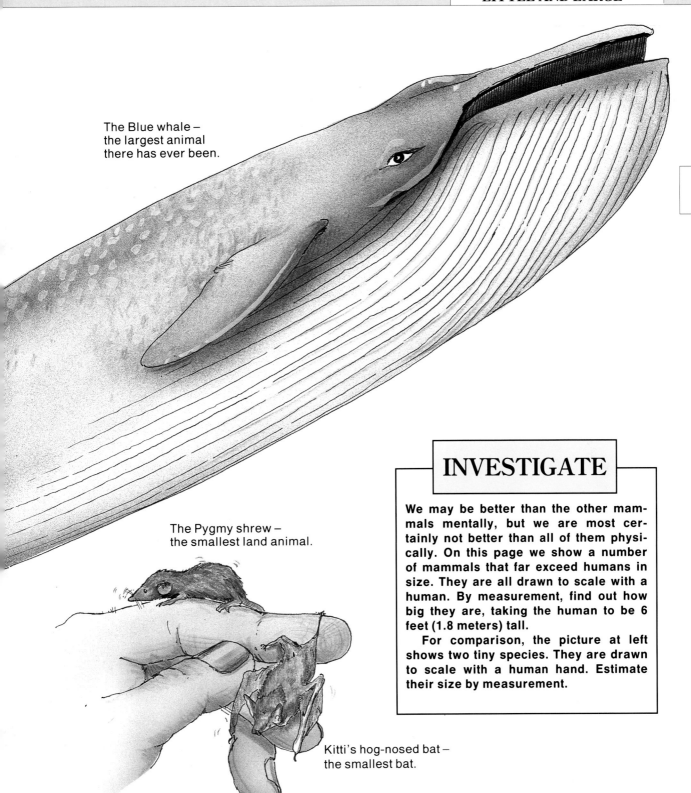

The Blue whale –
the largest animal
there has ever been.

The Pygmy shrew –
the smallest land animal.

Kitti's hog-nosed bat –
the smallest bat.

INVESTIGATE

We may be better than the other mammals mentally, but we are most certainly not better than all of them physically. On this page we show a number of mammals that far exceed humans in size. They are all drawn to scale with a human. By measurement, find out how big they are, taking the human to be 6 feet (1.8 meters) tall.

For comparison, the picture at left shows two tiny species. They are drawn to scale with a human hand. Estimate their size by measurement.

3 Animals in Their Habitats

◀ Polar bears playing in the water. These magnificent beasts, which can weigh up to nearly half a ton (450 kg), are now endangered because humans have hunted them and disturbed ther natural habitat.

▼ This nine-banded armadillo is common in the southern United States. Sometimes it curls itself into a ball.

Q Does it curl up when it goes to sleep, when it is attacked, or when it wants to roll down a slope?

All the many different kinds of animals – birds, mammals, and so on – are to be found all over the world. But a particular species of bird, mammal, and so on, is not found all over. Usually it can be found only in a certain region, where it is suited to the conditions there. The kind of conditions in which an animal lives is called its habitat.

The main thing that decides what a habitat is like is the climate, in particular the temperature and the amount of rainfall. Different plants grow in different climates, and these plants support different species of animals.

In this chapter we look at the animals that we can observe in a variety of different habitats throughout the world, and see how well they are adapted to these conditions. We look at animals of the prairies and savanna, woodland and forests, wetlands and deserts, polar regions and seashores.

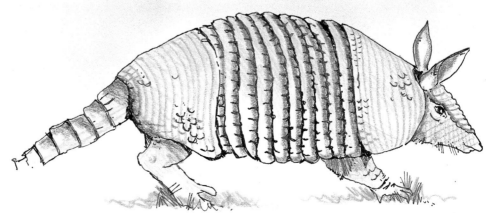

▶ The Florida Everglades covers more than 3,000 square miles (5,000 sq km) in total. One of the world's foremost wetland areas, it is a paradise for the naturalist.

▼ The open-air Sonora Desert Museum in Arizona was founded in 1952. It has on display in their natural outdoor setting more than 200 different animals and 400 kinds of plants. They represent the fauna and flora in the surrounding desert area.

Investigating animal life

Animals of one kind or another are all around us – in the countryside and garden, the city park and street, even in the home. Not all animals are welcome, of course! Many, such as cockroaches and rats, are absolute pests and can be harmful by spreading disease. However, the majority of animals don't bother us if we don't bother them.

All animals are worth watching and studying to investigate their habits and lifestyles. We can study them a little every day, wherever we are. But animal study becomes more exciting if we take a trip to an unfamiliar area with different wildlife. You may well already have been on several "field trips" at school, where you have done some serious wildlife studies.

The U.S. is such a vast country that it contains most kinds of habitats. This means that there is a huge variety of animal life scattered around that can be watched and studied.

The country is also well endowed with national park areas such as the Florida Everglades, and open-air museums such as the Sonora Desert Museum near Tucson, Arizona. Most have visitors' centers where experienced staff and rangers can advise and brief you about the local wildlife. They often have slide and film presentations about it, too.

What to take with you

Notebook
Record your observations, make sketches.

Binoculars
Take you close-up to wildlife without disturbing it; essential for serious study.

Camera
Essential for making a record of your trip; backs up observations.

Hand lens
Lets you investigate small creatures, such as bugs and beetles.

Knapsack
Needed to carry your odds and ends, which should include containers to hold small specimens and emergency rations of food and drink!

Clothing
Dress sensibly for the type of countryside you are in and for the time of year.

Field guides
Don't go without them! They are designed to help you identify wildlife on the spot.

The prairies

Vast grassy plains are found in several parts of the world in temperate climates that are not too hot, not too cold, and have a reasonable amount of rainfall. Under such conditions, grass grows well. These grassland regions are the natural home of the herbivores, or grazing animals.

In North America there is such a region east of the Rocky Mountains called the Great Plains. It streatches for hundreds of miles from the southern U.S. and north into Canada. It is often called the prairie. But because of farming, only a fraction of the original prairie remains.

Similar grassy plains exist in Argentina, where they are called the pampas; and in Russia, where they are called the steppe.

Q 1. Why is the prairie ideal for growing grain such as wheat and barley?

Where the buffalo roam

The most important native grazers of the prairie were the buffalo and the pronghorn antelope. Before the coming of the railroad and settlements, these animals roamed the prairies by the millions. But both species

Animals of the North American prairie. Buffaloes have again begun to flourish on the prairie under protection, and now number nearly 50,000. Large herds of pronghorns have also become well established and are now numbered in hundreds of thousands.

Q 2. The pronghorn is the swiftest of North America's animals. How fast do you think it can run: 23, 33, 43, 53, 63, 73 mph (37, 53, 85, 101, 117 km/h)?

Pronghorn

Prairie dogs

Buffalo

were hunted almost to extinction in the 1800s. Thankfully, under protection, their populations have recovered to reasonable numbers.

Among the smaller animals, prairie dogs are common. They burrow into the ground, making a network of tunnels and chambers. They are very sociable animals, often living together in "cities," or coteries, covering 100 acres (40 hectares) or more.

Q Prairie dogs aren't dogs. What animal family do you think they belong to?

On the savanna

In Africa the great grassy plains are known as the savanna. They are home to the largest concentrations of wild animals left on Earth. The climate of the savanna is hot and dry for about half the year and hot and wet for the other half.

The savanna boasts an extraordinary variety of animal life. The lion is the top meat-eating predator, feeding on zebra, wildebeest, and other grazers. Giraffe, elephant, and rhinoceroses (now increasingly rare) are among the other distinctive kinds of wildlife.

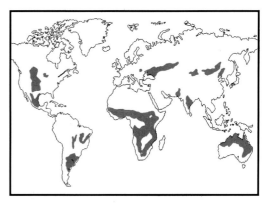

▲ This map shows the main prairie and savanna regions of the world.

43

Life on the African savanna is rich and varied. Two kinds of rhinoceroses are found, the Black and the White. The White tips the scales at over 2½ tons (2 tonnes). The savanna boasts the tallest animal, the giraffe, and the largest bird, the ostrich.

Ostrich

Lions

Giraffe

Zebra

Rhinoceros

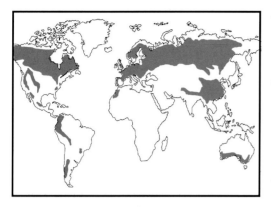

▲ This map shows the main woodland and cool forest regions of the world.

▼ Some animals of the deciduous woodlands. Foxes and martens are cunning predators, foxes on the ground and martens in the trees, where they often prey on squirrels. The skunk is another predator, belonging to the weasel family. The one in the picture is doing a handstand, warning that it is about to "fire" its foul-smelling spray.

44

Woodlands and forests

The world was once much more heavily forested than it is today. And over most of the United States, for example, only scattered woodlands remain. The typical trees of the woodlands are deciduous, which means they shed their leaves in the fall. The leaves grow again in the spring. Common woodland trees are beech, poplar, and maple.

Manmade forests are usually planted with the faster growing evergreen trees. These are trees like pine and fir, which have narrow, needle-like leaves and bear their seeds in cones. Vast regions of natural evergreen forest occur in northern North America, and also in northern Europe and Asia.

Q What are cone-bearing trees called?

Red squirrel

Pine marten

Red fox

Skunk

Pigeons

IT'S AMAZING!

Dormice may hibernate for up to nine months a year. Their temperature may drop nearly to freezing point. Their breathing and heart beat slow down so much that they hardly seem to be alive.

Life in the forest

Forests teem with life. Birds abound, from tits and warblers to treecreepers and woodpeckers. Ants forage in the leaf litter; so do groundhogs and badgers. Squirrels and martens hunt for food in the branches. Both like nuts, and martens like squirrels!

The gray squirrel is found in vast numbers over a wide range, in parks as well as in forests, and is a pest causing considerable damage to young trees. The red squirrel is much less bold, and tends to live in the heart of pine woods.

In cooler northern forest regions of North America, beavers are among the most interesting animals. They are the engineers of the animal world, felling trees and using them to build dams across streams. Among the largest animals in the forest are the elk, caribou, and moose. The forest offers protection for these and other animals during the harsh snowy winters.

Some animals, such as squirrels, may hibernate, or sleep through the winter. Squirrels do not sleep so deeply, waking up now and again to feed on nuts they have stored – if they can find them!

45

▼ **Some animals of the cool northern evergreen forests of North America. The moose is a magnificent beast, and is the world's largest deer. The males have splendid antlers with a span of up to 6 feet (1.8 meters).**

Moose

Beaver

Racoon

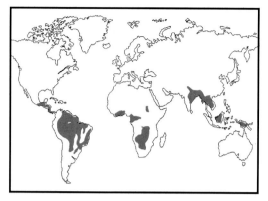

▲ **This map shows the main rain forest regions of the world.**

Rain forests

We tend to think of rain forests as occurring only in tropical regions near the Equator. But there are in fact some rain forests in the United States. They are located near the west coast, from northern California through Oregon, into Washington State.

The forests in this region are temperate rain-forests. They are cooler than the tropical ones, but still provide excellent growing conditions for trees, such as the mighty California redwoods, which are among the biggest and oldest living things on Earth.

Interesting animals of these rain forests include the American black bear and the Black-tailed, or Mule, deer. The porcupine is a prickly forest-dweller, usually found in trees. It causes a lot of damage in the forests because of its fondness for eating bark. Usually, the long quills on its back lie flat, but when it is threatened, they stand up. They can inflict nasty injuries when they get into another animal's flesh.

Temperate rain forests are also found on the other side of the Pacific Ocean, notably in New Zealand. In these forests lives the country's national bird, the flightless kiwi.

Q What is the alternative name of the Black-tailed deer, and why do you think it got that name?

Porcupine

Some animals of the temperate rain forest region on the west coast of the United States.

Black bear

Black-tailed deer

Tropical rain forests

The biggest regions of rain forest in the world girdle the Equator. They are the tropical rain forests, in which temperatures can average up to 80°F (27°C) all through the year. In these forests rain falls most days and can average up to 200 inches (5 meters) a year.

These very warm and very moist conditions allow plant life to flourish. The typical vegetation occurs in a number of layers. At the top is a dense leafy canopy, which forms an almost unbroken covering over the forest.

An astonishing variety of species lives in the varied habitats provided by the layers. The picture shows some of the animals found in the rain forests of South America.

Q Rain forests contain a greater abundance and variety of animal life than any other habitat. Why is this? Why is the forest floor generally quite dark?

▲ **The orang-utan is one of our closest relatives in the animal kingdom. It lives in the rain forests on the islands of Sumatra and Borneo in Southeast Asia.**

Macaw

Black howler monkey

Jaguar

Boa constrictor

Giant anteater

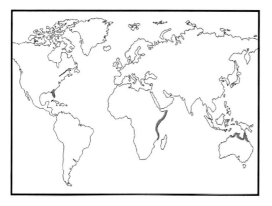

▲ This map shows the main wetland regions of the world.

▼ You can see plenty of turtles in the Florida Everglades, and you may be lucky enough to spot a Bald eagle. Thanks to complete protection, the Bald eagle is increasing in numbers.

Spoonbill

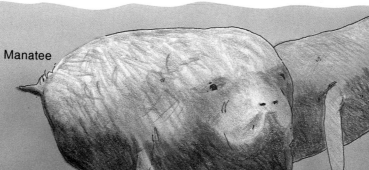

Manatee

Rivers, ponds, and wetlands

Rivers and ponds provide a freshwater habitat for many creatures near, on and below the surface. They have a complex food chain, which begins in the rotting vegetation on the bottom. This is eaten by numerous snails and tiny crustaceans such as freshwater shrimp. These are in turn eaten by fish, which in turn are taken by larger fish such as pike, and birds such as herons and egrets.

Swift flowing streams have less wildlife than still ponds, but they have some interesting inhabitants. One is the American dipper, which can be seen throughout North America. It is a small, plump bird that literally walks underwater head-down, probing for insects under stones on the stream-bed.

Q Which way do you think the dipper walks, upstream or downstream?

48

Sea cows and river horses

Birds are in general plentiful around rivers and ponds, as are amphibians such as frogs, toads, and newts. But mammals are scarcer, for water is not an obvious home for them. Among them are the rat-like water vole and that excellent swimmer, the otter.

A more exotic water-dweller is the manatee, or seacow, found in the warm rivers of the southern United States. It feeds on water weed. Other exotic species that prefer watery habitats include the hippopotamus ("river horse") of Africa.

The Everglades

In many parts of the world, freshwater stays on the ground rather than drain away into rivers. These areas are called swamps, or freshwater wetlands. The U.S. has several large expanses of such wetlands – the Great Dismal Swamp in North Carolina and Virginia, and the Great Cypress Swamp and the Everglades in Florida.

The Everglades is one of the world's most outstanding wetlands, which is home for aligators, turtles, and rich birdlife, including bald eagles, Roseate spoonbills, and flamingoes.

Q What did the Native Indians call the Everglades?

IT'S AMAZING!

The platypus of Australia is a curious creature. It has the body of an otter and the bill of a duck. It is neither a bird nor a reptile, yet it lays eggs. When its eggs hatch, the tiny young crawl onto the mother's belly and suck milk from glands there. The duck-billed platypus is a primitive mammal.

49

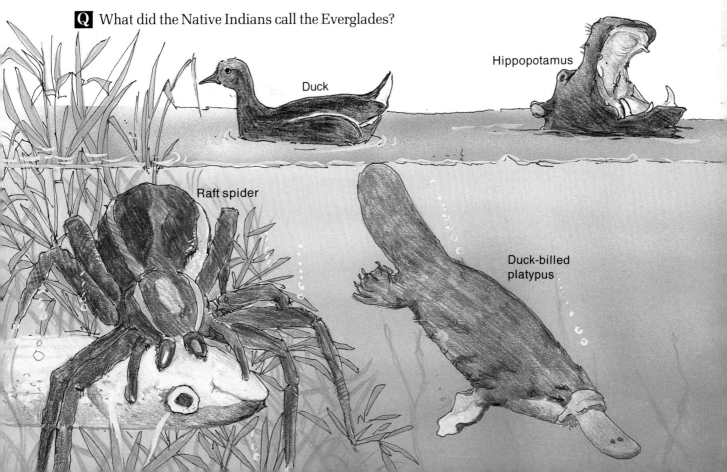

Hippopotamus

Duck

Raft spider

Duck-billed platypus

Scrub and desert

In the southwestern U.S. there are large areas of scrub and desert. The scrubland enjoys some rain during the mild winter, but virtually none during the very hot summers. In the deserts such as the Mojave and Sonora, little rain falls at any time of the year.

In California the scrubland is called the chapparal. It is home to a surprising number of animals, considering the harsh conditions. Several kinds of lizards live there, including the Western collared lizard and the Desert iguana.

The Antelope jack rabbit is a fleet-footed chapparal resident. It is noted for its huge ears. These help it keep cool by radiating away body heat. Along with other small animals, it is hunted by two of the region's "cats," the bobcat and the puma, or mountain lion. But the puma prefers to feed on larger prey, such as deer, if it can.

A distinctive bird of the scrub, which prefers to run rather than fly, is the road runner. It is a member of the cuckoo family.

Q What are cuckoos best known for?

50

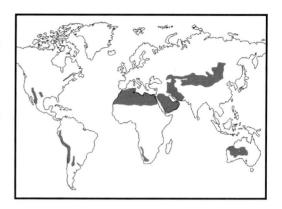

▲ This map shows the main scrub and desert regions of the world.

Some of the distinctive animals that inhabit the scrubland in California known as the chapparal.

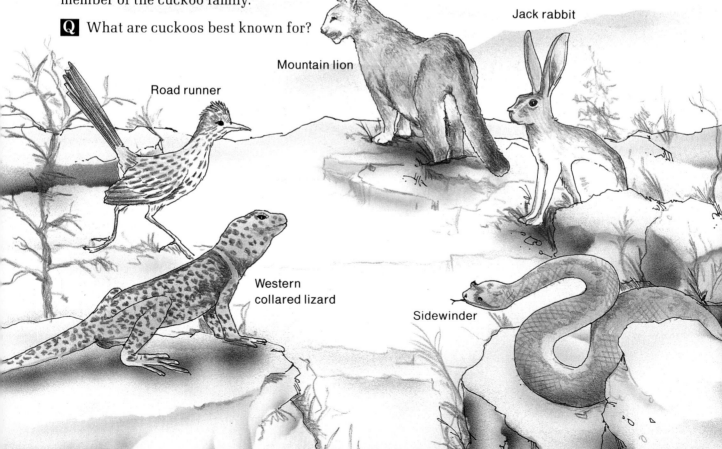

Jack rabbit

Mountain lion

Road runner

Western collared lizard

Sidewinder

Desert rats

In desert regions temperatures can soar to blistering heights. In Death Valley, for example, they often reach over 120°F (49°C). In such temperatures, much of the wildlife rests in the shade or in burrows during the day, and goes foraging for food in the cool of the night.

The desert residents are well adapted for life there. The Kangaroo rat, which lives in the western deserts of the U.S., never drinks water. It seems to get enough moisture for its body from the seeds it eats. Along with other desert rodents in other parts of the world, such as jerboas and gerbils, it produces only tiny drops of concentrated urine, thus conserving its body fluid.

Q **1.** Deserts are noted for their very high temperatures. What else are they noted for?

▲ **Death Valley, one of the hottest places on Earth. You can see little, if any, wildlife in this parched, rocky, desert wilderness during the day. Only in the comparative cool of the night do lizards, rodents, and other creatures emerge to feed.**

Q **1. The Arabian camel stores water in its hump. True or false?**

2. The Fennec fox of northern Africa has big ears that let it listen for beetles burrowing under the sand. True or false?

3. The Great gerbil of the Middle East and Asia drinks when it eats. It feeds on seeds at night when they are covered with dew. True or false?

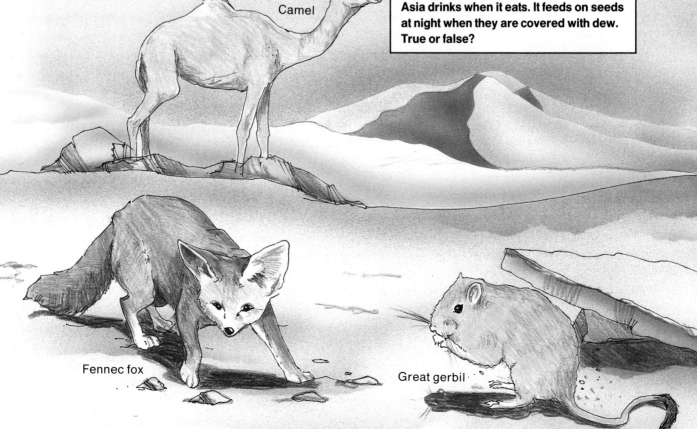

Camel

Fennec fox

Great gerbil

Cold climates

The coldest climates on Earth are found near the North and South Poles. In these polar regions, temperatures in the long winters can fall to below −80°F (−60°C) and howling winds create blinding blizzards. But even in these in hospitable places, there is animal life.

The region around the North Pole is called the Arctic. There is no land near the Pole itself, only ocean – the Arctic Ocean – which is largely covered by ice. Around the Ocean in the north of Alaska and Canada, and in northern Europe and Asia, is a region known as the tundra. It is not quite so cold as at the Pole itself, and it supports a varied animal population.

The tundra lies north of the great northern forest belt (see page 44). And during the brief Arctic summer, many of the forest residents roam onto the tundra to graze the sudden flush of vegetation. They include herds of caribou and moose. Following these herds are predators such as wolves, wolverines, and Brown bears. Great flocks of birds migrate to the Arctic tundra in summer, too, particularly geese such as Snow and White-fronted geese.

Some of the distinctive wildlife of the polar regions – around the North Pole (below) and the South Pole (opposite). One creature that can be found in both polar regions at different times of the year is the Arctic tern. The terns nest on the tundra in the brief Arctic summer, then fly south to the Antarctic, returning to the Arctic to nest again. This is a round trip of up to 22,000 miles (35,000 km)!

52

Musk oxen

Polar bear

Seal

Caribou

Arctic fox

Arctic hare

IT'S AMAZING!

The continent of Antarctica is covered by ice up to 2½ miles (4km) thick!

Tundra residents

The largest animals that remain on the tundra all year round are Musk oxen. They grow thick shaggy coats and have thick layers of body fat under the skin to protect them during the bitter winters.

Arctic foxes prey on Arctic hares throughout the year. The foxes often stray onto the pack ice, following the most formidable beasts in the Arctic, the Polar bears. These bears spend most of their time on the pack ice, hunting their favorite food, seals.

Q 1. The Arctic hare and Arctic fox have a brownish coat in summer, which changes to white in winter. Why do you think their color changes?

In the Antarctic

At the opposite end of the Earth is the south polar region, which is called the Antarctic. Here there is land, the continent of Antarctica. The animal life in Antarctica is concentrated around the edge of the continent. The most distinctive creatures are the penguins. The largest species is the Emperor. The Emperor penguin male incubates the single egg its mate lays by carrying it around on its feet and keeping it warm under a flap of skin.

Q 2. Penguins' wings don't look like those of other birds. They are shaped like flippers. What does this tell you about these birds?

53

Arctic tern

Emperor penguin

Rockhopper

Adélie

Shore life

In many respects the coastal regions of the world make a difficult habitat for many animals because of the presence of saltwater. This also limits the kinds of plants that can grow there. Nevertheless, the seashore and marshy areas nearby teem with life.

On the shore itself, which is periodically covered and uncovered by the sea, resident animal life is restricted mainly to relatively low life forms. Various worms and mollusks such as clams live on sandy and muddy shores, along with crustaceans such as crabs and the tiny sandhoppers. Mollusks such as limpets and whelks live on rocky shores. Their shells prevent their bodies from drying out when they are out of the water.

Q Why is the seashore "periodically covered and uncovered by the sea?"

54

Cormorant

Limpets

Mussels

Ragworm

IT'S AMAZING!

One of the strangest creatures of the shoreline is a fish called the mudskipper, which lives in the mangrove swamps of southeastern Asia. When the tide goes out, it often "skips" over the mud and climbs up a mangrove root, using its strong, muscular fins as "legs." Unlike most fish, it can breathe in air.

Bird life

Worms, mollusks, and crustaceans provide an abundant source of food for wading birds such as the little sandpiper and the larger and distinctive black and white avocets. The shore is also the home for many varieties of gulls and terns, which feed mainly offshore but also scavenge on shore. Gulls, such as the Herring gull, also venture inland to feed on garbage dumps.

In winter, the birdlife on the shores and coastal mudflats of the U.S. expands enormously. The resident populations are swelled by birds such as the Snow goose, migrating south to escape the Arctic winter. Other birds migrate to the coasts to enjoy the milder weather there.

Q Why is the weather on the coast usually milder than it is inland?

Some of the varied creatures that live in the difficult habitat of the seashore. There is an abundance of bird life on most shores, particularly gulls, of which there are more than 40 species. One of the American species, Bonaparte's gull, is unusual in that it nests in trees. The Californian gull nests far inland and is revered in Salt Lake City, Utah, for having saved the crops of the early Mormon settlers by eating the locusts that threatened to devour them.

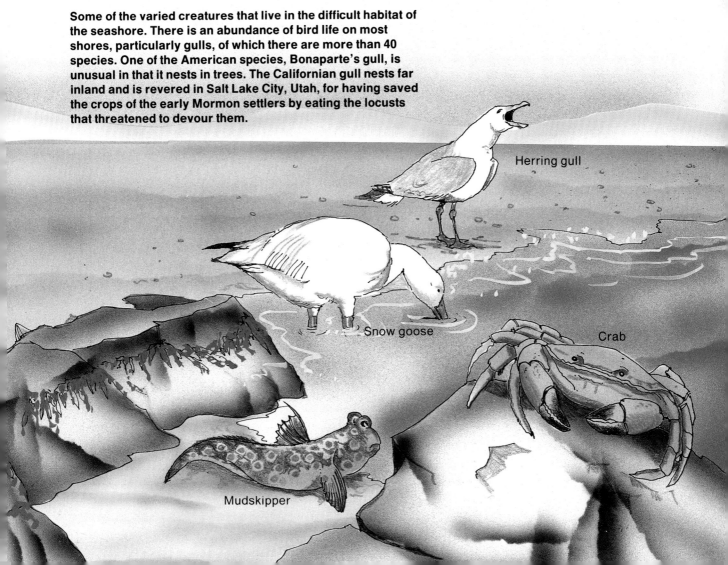

Herring gull

Snow goose

Crab

Mudskipper

Millions of Years Ago	Time Span	
1,200		The first animals appear on Earth, single-celled creatures called protozoa.
Up to 590	Precambrian Era	Only scant traces of life found in the rocks.
590-248	Palaeozoic Era	The era of ancient life, divided into six periods.
590-505	Cambrian Period	An "explosion" of life occurs. Invertebrates and mollusks became common in the seas.
504-438	Ordovician Period	Fish-like creatures appear.
437-408	Silurian Period	Giant sea scorpions live in the oceans.
407-360	Devonian Period	Fish become common, and the first amphibians appear.
359-286	Carboniferous Period	Reptiles develop and insects become large.
285-248	Permian Period	Reptiles become common and take many forms.
247-65	Mesozoic Era	The era of middle life, divided into three periods.
247-213	Triassic Period	The first, quite small, dinosaurs appear.
212-144	Jurassic Period	Dinosaurs of huge dimensions develop; other reptiles dominate the seas, even the air; the ancestors of birds appear.
143-65	Cretaceous Period	Dinosaurs with body "armor" and horns develop. But all are wiped out, with many other species, by a natural catastrophe at the end of this period.
64 - present day	Cenozoic Era	The era of recent life, divided into two periods.
64-2	Tertiary Period	Divided into five "epochs."
64-55	Paleocene Epoch	Small mammals, with warm blood and hair, become common.
54-38	Eocene Epoch	Modern species of mammals first appear, including ancestors of the horse, rhinoceros and elephant.
37-25	Oligocene Epoch	The ancestors of modern mammals become dominant; most ancient, primitive species die out.
24-5	Miocene Epoch	The first apes appear in Africa and Asia, including the direct ancestors of humans.
4-2	Pliocene Epoch	Mammals such as the elephant and horse begin to assume their modern form. In Africa man-apes became ape-men and began using tools; they were shaping up to become the dominant species on Earth.
2 - present day	Quaternary period	Divided into two epochs.
2 -10,000 years ago	Pleistocene Epoch	A time of repeated ice ages, during which mammoths, giant sloths, sabre-toothed tigers and other large mammals lived in many parts of the world. Human beings spread into Europe and North America.
10,000 years ago - present day	Holocene Epoch	Human beings become the dominant life form, hunting other animals species, then domesticating some for livestock.

Glossary

ADAPTATION   Features of an animal's body or way of life that make it fit in with its environment.

AMPHIBIANS   Broadly speaking, animals that are able to live in water and on land. More specifically, amphibians are a class of animals, including frogs and toads, which need water to breed in, although the adults live largely on land.

ANTARCTIC   The very cold region around the South Pole.

AQUATIC   Living for much, if not all, of the time in water.

ARBOREAL   Living for much, if not all, of the time in trees.

ARCTIC   The very cold region around the North Pole.

ARTHROPODS   Animals that have jointed legs, such as insects, mites and spiders.

BIG CATS   Large carnivores, such as lions, tigers, jaguars and leopards.

BIOLOGY   The science of living things.

BROWSING   Feeding on the shoots, leaves and bark of shrubs and trees.

BUDDING   A method of reproduction used by certain primitive water animals, such as the hydra.

CAMOUFLAGE   The pattern, color or shape of an animal that enables it to blend in with its surroundings and hide, usually for protection.

CARNIVORES   In general, animals that feed on the flesh of other animals; meat-eaters. More specifically, animals that belong to the class of carnivores, such as dogs, cats and bears.

CANOPY   The upper layer of forest, formed by interlacing branches and leaves.

CARRION   The flesh of dead animals.

CARTILAGE   Soft gristly tissue that forms the skeleton of some animals, such as sharks.

CELL   The smallest body unit.

CHAPPARAL   A large region of scrubland in California.

COLD-BLOODED ANIMALS   Ones that have the same temperature as their surroundings, such as snakes and lizards.

COMPOUND EYE   The kind of eye insects have, which consists of thousands of separate little lenses.

CONIFER TREES   Ones that bear their seeds in cones. They are usually evergreen and have needle-like leaves.

CRUSTACEANS   Animals with jointed legs and a hard outer shell, such as crabs, scorpions and lobsters.

CUD   The ball of food ruminants brought back from the stomach to the mouth for chewing.

DECIDUOUS TREES   Trees that shed all their leaves at once, usually in the fall.

DESERT   A region that has little, if any, rainfall during the year. Most deserts are very hot.

DNA   The substance in the nucleus of a cell that controls all cell functions. DNA is short for deoxyribonucleic acid.

57

58

ENVIRONMENT The surroundings, including physical features, climate, and living things.

EQUATOR An imaginary line around the Earth midway between the North and South Poles.

FAUNA Animal life.

FERTILIZATION The coming together of male and female sex cells to create new life.

FORAGE Go in search of food.

GENUS The division in animal classification above Species and below Family.

GRAZING Feeding on grass.

HABITAT The kind of surroundings in which an animal lives.

HERBIVORES Animals that eat plants.

HERMAPHRODITES Animals that have both male and female sex organs.

HIBERNATION Winter sleep.

INCUBATION Sitting on eggs to keep them warm so that the young can develop inside.

INSECTIVORES Insect-eaters, such as bats and hedgehogs.

INVERTEBRATES Animals without a backbone, such as insects and snails.

LARVA An early stage in the development of an animal, such as an insect or amphibian.

MAMMALS The most advanced animal class, in which the females feed their young on milk from their bodies.

MANGROVES Trees that grow on the muddy shores of river deltas and estuaries in warm climates.

MARINE Living in the sea.

MARSUPIALS Primitive mammals that bear undeveloped young. The young usually mature in pouches in the mother's body.

METAMORPHOSIS The change in body form some animals undergo when they develop from egg to adult.

MOLLUSKS A class of animals that usually have hard shells, such as snails; though some, such as octopuses, have a kind of shell inside their bodies, instead of outside.

NOCTURNAL Active during the night.

OMNIVORE An animal that eats both animals and plants.

PARASITE An animal that lives on another (a host) and feeds on it, such as a flea.

PAMPAS The temperate grassland regions in South America.

PLACENTA An organ in female mammals that channels food to the developing young.

PRAIRIE The temperate grassland regions in North America.

PREDATOR An animal that hunts other animals for food.

PREY An animal that is hunted for food.

PRIMATES The order of mammals to which we belong, together with monkeys and apes.

PROTOZOA Animals made up of a single cell.

RAIN FOREST Tropical and subtropical forest close to the equator, which receives plentiful rainfall all through the year.

REPRODUCTION   An essential characteristic of animal (and plant) life: that an animal can reproduce its own kind, or in other words, have offspring.

REPTILES   Scaly-skinned animals such as alligators, snakes, and lizards. They are cold blooded.

RESPIRATION   The process by which animals take in oxygen to "burn" their food and give out carbon dioxide as a waste product.

RODENTS   An order of mammals to which rats, mice, and squirrels belong.

RUMINANTS   Animals that "chew the cud," such as cattle and deer. They have a many-chambered stomach to assist the digestion of tough plant tissues.

SAVANNA   Tropical grassland, especially that in eastern and southern Africa.

SCRUB   A hot, dry region with low, shrubby vegetation.

SENSES   The means by which animals take in information about the world around them.

SPECIES   In general, species means kind. But more specifically, species is the division in animal classification below genus. Scientifically, an animal (or a plant) is named by its genus and species. The scientific name for the beaver, for example, is *Castor canadiensis – Castor* being the genus, *canadiensis* the species.

STEPPE   The temperate grassland regions of eastern Europe and Asia.

TEMPERATE CLIMATE   One that is not too hot and not too cold and that has a reasonable amount of rainfall.

TROPICS   A region with a hot climate on either side of the Equator. Strictly speaking, it is the region between latitude 23 ½° North (the Tropic of Cancer) and latitude 23 ½° South (the Tropic of Capricorn).

TUNDRA   The very cold treeless wilderness in far northern regions of North America, Europe, and Asia.

VERTEBRATES   Animals that have backbones, such as fish, amphibians, reptiles, birds, and mammals.

WARM-BLOODED ANIMALS   Ones that can maintain a steady body temperature independent of the temperature of its surroundings. All birds and mammals are warm blooded.

WETLANDS   Regions where water lays on the surface for most of the time, such as esturies, mud flats, and swamps.

ZOOLOGY   The scientific study of animals.

Answers

Page 9

An animal that eats meat is called a carnivore.

Page 16

1. The tarsier is a nocturnal animal. It has huge eyes so that it can see well in the dark. Then its pupils open wide to gather the maximum amount of light.

2. Cats' eyes are usually green, except for some breeds, for example, Siamese, which have blue eyes. But all cats and members of the cat family have eyes with vertical pupils.

Page 17

1. The mouse uses its whiskers to extend its sense of touch.

2. The moth uses its antennae to detect smells. It can detect moth smells over a distance of several miles.

Page 21

Whales belong to the animal group, mammals.

Page 24

Investigation

Day by day you will see the worms making tunnels. They drag the leaves and grass down below the surface and churn up the layers until all the material in the the worm farm looks the same. This is what they do in the soil.

Page 25

These mollusks propel themselves through the water by jet propulsion. They take water into their bodies and then squirt it out. This jet action propels them in the opposite direction.

Page 27

1. Insects play a major role in the plant world by pollinating the flowers, that is, carrying pollen from one flower to another, thereby bringing abou fertilization.

2. If you look in the picture, you can see that the mites have four pairs of legs. Therefore they are not insects, which have only three pairs.

Page 28

Insects have just six legs; the other arthropods have more. Millipedes have as many as 150!

Page 30

1. Because reptiles are cold-blooded, they need to take in heat from their surroundings before they can become active. This can't happen in cold climates.

2. Young will develop inside eggs only if the eggs are kept warm. Cold-blooded animals can't supply the warmth.

Page 31

The "terrible lizards" were the dinosaurs, which dominated the world for over 150 million years before they died out about 65 million years ago.

Page 33

The correct labels should be:
(A) Wading, **(B)** Swimming, **(C)** Perching, and **(D)** Fishing.

Page 36

The largest dinosaurs, the brachiosaurs, measured up to about 87 feet (26.5 meters) long.

The Blue whale can measure up to 100 feet (33 meters) or more and weigh up to 210 tons (190 tonnes).

The African elephant, on average, stands up to 10.5 feet (3.2 meters) at the shoulder and weighs about 6.5 tons (6 tonnes).

The pygmy shrew can measure as little as 2.4 inches (6 cm) long and weigh as little as one-twentieth of an ounce (1.5 grams)

Kitti's hog-nosed bat has a wingspan of about 6 inches (15 mm) and is fractionally heavier than the pygmy shrew.

The odd animal out in the picture is the dinosaur. Dinosaurs were reptiles, not mammals.

Page 41
The armadillo rolls up when it is attacked. Its "armor plate" protects it well.

Page 42
1. The prairie provides ideal growing conditions for wheat and other grain because they all belong to the grass family.
2. The pronghorn can reach 53 mph (85 km/h).

Page 43
Prairie dogs belong to the squirrel family. They are a kind of ground squirrel.

Page 44
Cone-bearing trees are called conifers.

Page 46
The Mule deer is named for its large furry ears, which resemble those of a mule.

Page 47
Because of the hot and moist conditions, the plants in the forest grow, flower, and fruit continuously throughout the year, providing an abundance of food for animals. The forest floor is dark because the dense canopy lets through little light.

Page 49
American Indians called the Everglades "Grassy Waters," which is an excellent name. It is really a vast, shallow, slowly moving river.

Page 50
Ordinary cuckoos are known for their distinctive call "Cuck-Coo" and for the habit they have of laying eggs in other birds' nests. The road runner, however, does not do this.

Page 51
Deserts are noted for their very high temperatures and their lack of water.
Box
1. False. The camel does not store water in its hump. It conserves water by hardly sweating at all.
2. True. The Fennec fox does use its ears to listen for beetles, but they also help it stay cool by radiating away the body heat.
3. Partly true. The Great gerbil does get the water its body needs from the seeds it eats, whether or not they are covered by dew.

Page 53
1. The Arctic hare and Arctic fox change their color for camouflage. The brownish coat helps them blend with the vegetation during the summer, and the white coat blends with the snow during winter.
2. Penguins can't fly but they are expert swimmers. They use their flipper-like wings to propel themselves through the water.

Page 54
The shore is "periodically covered and uncovered" because of the twice-daily ebbing and flowing of the tides.

For Further Reading

Crump, Donald J.
How Animals Behave.
National Geographic, Washington DC. 1984.

Freedman, Russell.
Can Bears Predict Earthquakes? : Unsolved Mysteries of Animal Behaviour.
Prentice-Hall, Eaglewood Cliffs, NJ. 1982.

Johnson, Rebecca L.
The Secret Language: Pheremones in the Animal World.
Lerner, Minneapolis, MN. 1989.

Koebner, Linda.
For Kids Who Love Animals: A Guide to Sharing the Planet.
Living Planet Press, San Francisco, CA. 1991.

Maynard, Thans.
Animal Inventors.
Franklin Watts, New York, 1991.

Nielson, Nancy J.
Animal Migration.
Franklin Watts, New York, 1991.

Quiri, Patricia R.
Metamorphosis.
Franklin Watts, New York, 1991.

Satler, Helen R.
Fish Facts and Bird Brains: Animal Intelligence.
Dutton, New York. 1984.

Steffens, Bradley.
Animal Rights: Distinguishing Between Fact and Opinion.
Greenhaven, St. Paul, MN. 1990.

Taylor, Dave.
Endangered Forest Animals.
Crabtree Publishers, New York, 1992.

Picture Credits

The publisher gratefully acknowledges the
following for providing the pictures in this book.
Sdeuard C. Bisserot: 6-7, 8, 20, 30, 31, 34, 47
Graham Beehag Books: 12
Robin Kerrod: 27, 33, 40, 48, 51
Frank Lane Picture Library: 13
Marwell Zoological Park: Title page, 35, 38

Index

63